DAVID PURDY is a social econon
of the Department of Applied
Manchester. Politically active
member of Democratic Left Scotland and lives in Stirling. Since
1991, he has spent several periods as a Visiting Research Fellow
at the European University Institute in Florence and has published
on various aspects of European economic and social policy
including, most recently:

> (2001) 'Economic Theory and Policy from the Keynesian
> Revolution to the Third Way' in Lars Magnusson and Bo
> Strath (eds) *From Werner Plan to EMU: In Search of a*
> *Political Economy for Europe*, (Brussels: PIE-Peter Lang),
> pp 97–124.

> (2001) 'Welfare Reform, Social Citizenship and European
> Integration', ibid., pp 389–411.

> (2001) 'Social Policy' in MJ Artis and FI Nixson (eds) *The*
> *Economics of the European Union* (3rd ed) (Oxford:
> Oxford University Press), pp 240-270.

Eurovision
or American Dream?

Britain, the Euro
and the Future of Europe

DAVID PURDY

Luath Press Limited

EDINBURGH

www.luath.co.uk

Published in association with

democratic left scotland

Democratic Left Scotland is a non-party political organization working for progressive social change through activity in civil society – in community groups, social movements and single-issue campaigns. DLS seeks to promote discussion and alliances across the lines of party, position and identity from a standpoint that is radical, feminist and green. Further information is available from:

Democratic Left Scotland
1A Leopold Place
Edinburgh EH7 5JW
Tel: 0131 477 2997
E-mail: dls@newpolitics.org.uk
Web: www.newpolitics.org.uk

First Published 2003

The paper used in this book is acid-free, neutral-sized and recyclable. It is made from low chlorine pulps produced in a low energy, low emission manner from sustainable forests.

Printed and bound by
Bell and Bain Ltd., Glasgow

Typeset in Sabon 10.5 by Sarah Crozier, Nantes

Acknowledgements

This book has been produced under the auspices of Democratic Left Scotland with the help of a grant from the Barry Amiel and Norman Melburn Trust. I am grateful to Jane Corrie, Pat Devine, Barbara MacLennan and Steve Matthewson for their comments on an earlier draft. The views expressed in the book, together with responsibility for any remaining errors, are entirely mine

Contents

Where there is no vision, the people perish.
(Proverbs, 29:18)

There is no such thing as free trade ...
You have to have rules of the road.
Mickey Kantor, US Trade Representative, 1993[1]

---

[1] Quoted in Dryden (1995) p387

Introduction: The Big Picture

PUBLIC DEBATE IN BRITAIN about the euro and future of the European Union (EU) has been insular, shallow and dull. This book offers a fresh approach to the issues. It is not another propaganda exercise, using slick words and slanted statistics in a bid to win votes at a future referendum. I am, in fact, in favour of joining the euro. But more importantly, I am convinced that, for all its faults, the EU is a good thing, not just for Britain, but for the world as a whole, because it offers possibilities that would not otherwise exist of preserving what is best in modern Europe, challenging the unlimited rule of global market forces and building a better world order. It is this big picture which has been so conspicuously and lamentably absent from the British debate.

The EU set out on the road to Economic and Monetary Union (EMU) when its Member States signed the Maastricht Treaty in December 1991, and four years have now elapsed since the twelve founding members of the euro-zone locked their exchange rates together, pending the advent of the euro in the material form of banknotes and coins. Time enough, one might have thought, for voters and parties in Britain to make up their minds about whether to scrap the pound and face up to the realities of life in the age of global capitalism. Yet popular debate about what may well be the most fateful decision voters will ever be called upon to take has scarcely begun, while politicians and pundits remain preoccupied with narrowly economic issues, weighing the benefits of the single currency for consumers and tourists against the costs of converting cash machines to a new monetary unit or the risks of an interest rate regime where 'one size fits all'. Perhaps Bonaparte was right, after all, and the English *are* a 'nation of shopkeepers'. Certainly, to the limited extent that politics has played any part in the national conversation, the alternatives have been crudely polarised: either a federal European Union or a sovereign United Kingdom.

Not that the economic arguments been properly considered either. Among the many issues excluded from Gordon Brown's famous 'five tests', for example, is the exchange rate at which Britain might join the euro. Given that for the past four years sterling has been overvalued against the euro and that going in at too high a rate would condemn the UK economy to years of slow growth until wages and prices became competitive again, this is a disturbing omission. Consider the historical precedents. In 1925, when Winston Churchill was Chancellor of the Exchequer, the decision was taken to return to the Gold Standard, suspended since the outbreak of the First World War, at the pre-war parity of $4.80 to the pound. Only this symbolic rate, it was believed, could convince investors and traders that 'business as usual' had resumed. Yet according to Keynes, the Treasury's insistence on 'looking the dollar in the face' overvalued the pound by about 10%, an estimate endorsed by most other economists then and since. The implication was that if the competitiveness of British goods on the international market was to be maintained, costs and prices would have to fall by about the same proportion, and since there was little scope for lowering costs in the short run by raising output per worker, the only remaining option was to cut workers' wages. This, warned Keynes in *The Economic Consequences of Mr. Churchill*, was a recipe for industrial strife and class war. At best, the policy would take years to work and, in the meantime, with production costs and selling prices slowly sagging downwards, business confidence would evaporate and the economy would sink deeper into recession.

The immediate result of the return to Gold was the General Strike of 1926. Five years later, a minority Labour government, stunned by the world-wide slump that followed the Wall Street Crash of 1929 and paralysed in the face of mass unemployment, was ignominiously bundled out of office after failing to halt a speculative run on the pound. Conventional wisdom insisted that the only way to restore confidence in the currency was to balance the budget by cutting public expenditure.[2] When the Cabinet balked at the prospect of cutting unemployment benefit, Ramsay MacDonald, the Labour Prime Minister, resigned and was immediately invited to form a 'National' government, dominated by the Conservatives. Within days of taking office, the new administration brought the crisis to an end by leaving the Gold Standard and devaluing the pound, though the advantage thus gained was soon lost as other governments promptly devalued *their* currencies in a bid to protect domestic industries and jobs. Worse was to come. 'Beggar-my-neighbour' remedies for unemployment were not just futile: by aggravating international tensions, they helped to bring the Nazis to power in Germany and set the world on the road to another war.

But if the stakes are so high, why has the debate been so poor? The decadence of our democracy has conspired with accidents of timing to produce a chronic state of ignorance, insularity and indecision. The British public knows less about the EU than the citizens of any other member state and mistrusts its own government to a degree surpassed only by the French.[3] For its part, a government notorious for being averse to risk and obsessed with control has made little attempt to win over a eurosceptical public for fear of stirring up the europhobic press. During its first term in office, New Labour attached overriding priority to establishing a reputation for economic competence, judging – correctly – that this was the best way to maintain business confidence, consolidate its electoral popularity and secure a second term. Thus the euro was not an issue and the five-test formula, devised in October 1997, served to keep it off the agenda.

---

[2] This was an early instance of what would now be called a 'fiscal crisis'. Contemporary manifestations include periodic newspaper headlines warning of the 'pensions time bomb' or announcing the discovery of a 'black hole' in Britain's public finances, and the shenanigans surrounding the 'Stability and Growth Pact' (discussed in Section 2).

[3] Eurobarometer Survey of EU Public Opinion, reported in *The Guardian*, 22.10.02

This strategic calculation was reinforced by the divergent development of the British and European economies. As Britain maintained the steady economic expansion that began in 1991–2, sterling appreciated against the Deutsche Mark. Conversely, until the euro was finally launched in 1999, the other big EU economies – France, Germany and Italy – experienced sluggish growth and mounting unemployment. This was due not to 'structural rigidities', as alleged by exponents of today's conventional wisdom, but to what might be called the 'Economic Consequences of Herr Kohl': the continuing fiscal burden imposed by Germany's over-hasty reunification, compounded by the deflationary impact of the Maastricht convergence criteria, the monetary and financial straitjacket designed by the German Bundesbank as the only basis on which it was prepared to countenance French plans for EMU. Fearful that German reunification might unhinge the EU, France sought to reconstitute the Franco-German axis around the project of monetary union and, to this end, was willing to let the Bundesbank dictate the terms. With the exception of Denmark and the UK, which opted out of EMU, other EU governments reluctantly fell into line for fear that if they did not, the EU would fall apart.[4][5]

Since the late 1990s, however, the British and European economic cycles have become more synchronised and, for what it is worth, most observers now agree that the five tests have been satisfied, though there remains the awkward problem of the exchange rate noted previously. (These matters are discussed in Section 2). Yet even before the Iraq war the odds against a referendum being held this side of the next General Election were lengthening, after a period in the early months of 2002, following the glitch-free introduction of the euro, when they had appeared

---

[4] Of the three countries which became members of the EU in 1995, Austria and Finland decided to opt into EMU, while Sweden joined Denmark and the UK in opting out.

[5] A brief, chronological account of the history of EMU is provided in Appendix 2.

to shorten. There has been much speculation about the reasons for this on-again, off-again pattern. Some detect latent flaws in the Blair–Brown duumvirate; others see only the froth of spin and hype.

But whatever the explanation, one point seems plain. When Tony Blair speaks of joining the euro in terms of 'national destiny', he is surely right about the *importance* of the issue for Britain. (It is important for Europe too, though less so. The members of the euro-zone would prefer Britain to join, but can rub along fairly well without us. How Britain would fare as a *permanent* outsider is less clear). The *significance* of the issue is another matter. 'Destiny' is a dangerous word and, certainly, a misleading one if it is taken to mean that – to coin a phrase – 'there is no alternative'. Quite apart from the fact that life goes on outside the single currency, there is more than one view about where Britain-in-Europe – or for that matter, Scotland-in-Europe – should be going. Nevertheless, entry into the euro-zone, if and when it happens, will be a defining moment in the nation's – and nations' – history, on a par, say, with the entry of the United States into the Second World War. While this by no means guaranteed an eventual Allied victory, it did reduce the chances of defeat. It also marked the beginning of Britain's 'special relationship' with the us as a dependent and subordinate partner.

Whether or not the New Labour government decides to hold a referendum on the euro before the next general election, wider questions about the shape and direction of the EU, including its role on the global stage, are likely to remain at the forefront of national and European politics over the next few years. Barring unforeseen events, in 2004, the fifteen established member states will be joined by a further ten – five in central Europe, the three Baltic States and Cyprus and Malta. Two more countries – Bulgaria and Romania – are preparing for entry at a later date, and accession negotiations with Turkey are due to begin in 2005. To accommodate its impending enlargement, the EU has launched a 'Convention on the Future of Europe', attended by 105 full delegates representing national governments and parliaments in both member states and candidate countries, as well as the European Commission and the European Parliament. The Convention's task is to review the institutions and governance of the EU and report to the European Council of Elected Heads of Government in May 2003 pending an intergovernmental, treaty-making conference the following year.

Besides paving the way for enlargement to the east, the Convention provides European leaders with a chance to reverse the unpopularity of the EU in the west. The situation is urgent for the chance may not come again and the EU faces a veritable crisis of legitimacy. Unless ways are found to restore people's faith in the European project, it is in danger of foundering in a backlash of disenchantment and xenophobia. And quite apart from its importance for the citizens of Europe, the process of enlargement and reform takes on a wider, global significance in a world where the American Empire is at odds with the EU over a whole range of issues, from steel tariffs and greenhouse gases to development aid and the Middle East. In the final section of the book, I argue that the EU offers opponents of neo-liberalism abundant, but as yet unused, scope for challenging US hegemony and bringing global capitalism under control, not by turning it into a rival superpower, but by drawing on the collectivist policy traditions of its member states, its experience of multi-tiered government, its international connections and the potential strength that comes from having a large market and a world currency, to promote new, transnational forms of economic and social regulation, cover-ing all the issues that today give rise to so much anger, fear and despair: the conduct of transnational companies, the system of international finance, the despoliation of the planet, the violation of human rights and the treatment of collapsed states. In this sense, 'anti-globalisers' are right to insist that 'another world is possible'. Where they are wrong is in supposing that a new and better world can somehow be built *outside* existing global institutions, on pure unsullied ground – a green-field site, perhaps – rather than contesting the present *form* of globalisation and working to reclaim the ground that has been lost over the past thirty years as the 'conservative' revolution has spread around the Earth from its home in the USA.

Whatever its eventual outcome, the Iraq war has shattered the old world order, sidelining the UN, splitting the EU and creating a precedent for further wars waged by *ad hoc* US-led coalitions in the name of regime change and the prevention of terrorism. As America's pivotal ally and chief accomplice, Britain has paid a high price in terms of moral obloquy, diplomatic isolation and estrangement from France and Germany, not to mention soldiers' lives and additional public expenditure. Britain's stance has also damaged the EU. By choosing to appease the Bush administration in the hope of exerting a moderating influence, rather than making common cause with its EU partners around an alternative global vision, the Blair government has spectacularly, if belatedly, vindicated General de Gaulle's warning that Britain was America's Trojan horse.

Of course, in one sense, Donald Rumsfeld's provocative distinction between the 'new' pro-American Europe and the 'old' Franco-German bloc is delusory. It rests on a crude conflation of states and citizens which is belied by the appeal of the slogan, 'Not in my name'. The scale of anti-war protest in Italy and Spain, for example, the two main continental European countries whose heads of government gave their backing to Bush and Blair surpassed even the unprecedented levels manifested in Britain before the start of the war put an end to any realistic hope of stopping it. But Rumsfeld's distinction serves not so much to describe the existing state of the world as to change it. In this sense, it is a weapon in the wider ideological and political conflict with which this book is concerned. For the time being, the invasion of Iraq has strengthened American hegemony and discomposed the forces ranged against it. But one war does not settle the fate of the world. It does not even settle the fate of one country. There is still time for Britain to change course, terminate the 'special relationship', repudiate neo-conservatism and take its place at the heart of a Europe dedicated to renewing the social rights of citizens, both within each state and throughout the world.

But this is to get ahead of the game. First, I need to review the arguments about whether Britain should join the euro. This is the task of Section 2. In Section 3, I discuss the issues raised by EU enlargement and reform, paying particular attention to a question that is almost never asked: namely, what is the EU for? In Section 4, I argue that recurrent collisions between the EU and the US are rooted in differences of history and culture, and that the much-vaunted 'clash of civilisations' runs not between 'authoritarian Islam' and 'democratic capitalism', but between two incompatible kinds of capitalism: the various socialised and regulated forms that have developed in Western Europe and the more feral variety that flourishes on the other side of the Atlantic. Finally, in Section 5, I consider what the EU can do to renew its social model, reconnect with its citizens and set about building a better world order. The proposals offered are illustrative and tentative. At this stage, it is more important to stake out a general line of advance than to devise a comprehensive and definitive programme. The task of remodelling European social capitalism and working towards a more balanced and diverse pattern of world development will take decades, just as it took decades to cage and tame the capitalist tiger on the terrain of the nation-state. This said, the present juncture in world politics, when options are still open and forces still fluid, will not last long. In that sense, we need to get a move on before it is too late.

David Purdy
April 2003

2

Should Britain Join the Euro?

FOR BETTER OR WORSE, the single currency now exists and the issue for Britain is no longer whether it is a good idea, but whether to join it. In judging this question, it needs to be borne in mind that a separate national currency is no guarantee of monetary autonomy. Nowadays, the monetary authorities of individual countries have little effective control over domestic interest rates and the foreign exchange rate. Suppose that a country wants to fix its exchange rate, either against a matrix of currencies, as in the old Exchange Rate Mechanism (ERM), or against the dollar, as in the international monetary system that prevailed from the end of the Second World War until 1971. The authorities will immediately set interest rates at whatever level is required to support the exchange rate chosen. But they must then reckon with the liquid global capital market that has developed over the past thirty years. In a world where money can move freely, quickly and on a scale that dwarfs the foreign exchange reserves held by national central banks, interest rates are driven up or down as speculators switch funds between currencies, putting irresistible pressure on a fixed exchange rate. The summary ejection of sterling from the ERM in September 1992 provides a recent case in point.

Thus, the choice for Britain lies between membership of the single currency and a fully floating exchange rate. The trouble with floating is that it creates uncertainty for companies which export or compete with imports: their production costs are incurred in sterling, but their selling prices and profits depend on the exchange rate, and it is not possible for them to insure themselves effectively against the risk of fluctuations. This problem would exist even if exchange rates moved in textbook fashion to compensate for differences in national inflation rates and the relative competitiveness of sectors engaged in external trade, as reflected in the current account of the balance of payments. But in practice, the sheer volume of cross-border capital flows and the herd-like behaviour of fund-holders make exchange rates volatile, frequently causing them to overshoot the changes that would be needed to bring about such adjustments: indeed, for years at a time they may move in the *opposite* direction to that required. Thus, a floating exchange rate itself becomes a source of economic disruption, rather than a means of offsetting it.

Again, Britain's recent experience is salutary. Between 1996 and 2000 the pound rose by 25% against the euro at a time when inflation was higher in Britain than in the other advanced capitalist countries and the current account of Britain's balance of payments was moving steadily from surplus to deficit. The sharp rise in the value of the pound made British goods more expensive on the international market, to the particular detriment of the manufacturing sector. The same thing happened in 1979-81 when sterling's newly acquired status as a petro-currency was reinforced by the Thatcher government's determination to beat inflation down by jacking interest rates up: hot money poured into London, causing the pound to appreciate and exacerbating the prevailing recession.

As long as Britain remains outside the euro, the disadvantage of floating will grow, for now that the single European currency exists Britain is more exposed to exchange rate risk than before. Within the euro-zone, producers face no currency risk, whereas UK firms selling in Europe continue to face uncertainty about the value of the pound and are under increasing pressure to set their prices in euro. Of course, joining the single currency will still leave Britain exposed to fluctuations in the euro-dollar rate. But since Britain exports three times as much to countries in the euro area as to the US, it is more important to have stability with the euro than with the dollar. Moreover, because the euro is a continental currency representing, on its current membership, about one sixth of world output, it will tend to be more stable against other world currencies – the dollar and the yen – than any national currency could be.

The Five Tests

Within Britain, public debate about whether to adopt the euro has revolved around Gordon Brown's famous five tests. These can be summarised as follows:

1. Have the British and European business cycles converged sufficiently?

2. Is Britain flexible enough to deal with any problems that may emerge?

3. Will membership help to promote long-term foreign investment in the UK?

4. Will membership be good for the UK financial services sector?

5. Will membership help to promote growth, stability and employment?

Ever since the tests were first formulated in 1997, the government has insisted that it favours joining the euro in principle, but will not authorise a referendum until there is 'clear and unambiguous evidence' that they have been met. Up to a point, this is a defensible position. There is nothing wrong with advocating membership of a currency union, while remaining cautious about the timing and exchange rate of entry; but only so long as a serious effort is made to inform and educate the public about the issues at stake. This New Labour has failed to do. Few people are familiar with the five tests which are, in any case, somewhat arbitrary. Why, for example, single out financial services for special mention, but ignore manufacturing? Nowadays, to be sure, the proportion of the workforce directly employed in this sector is less than a fifth and falling, but it still accounts for three quarters of the UK's 'visible' exports and for half its exports of merchandise and services combined. And why only *five* tests? What about the exchange rate at which sterling enters the euro, the remit and operating rules of the European Central Bank (ECB), the arrangements for holding the Bank to account and the budgetary regime enshrined in the Stability and Growth Pact (SGP), with which members of the euro-zone have pledged to comply?

The suggestion, peddled by the europhobic press, that the five tests are just window-dressing for a decision that has already been taken, is wide of the mark. Indeed, almost the opposite is true. The exacting standards imposed by the Treasury look more like crabbing caution than decisive leadership. In part, this is because Gordon Brown is proud of his record as Chancellor and does not want to put his reputation at risk by making the 'wrong' choice on the euro. In addition, the government is aware that although the eurosceptical majority consistently recorded by UK opinion polls is 'soft' and could be reversed by a determined political campaign, a referendum will be no walkover, especially if the economic arguments are in any way 'fudged'. This said, since economics is not a 'hard' science, least of all when applied to big decisions for which there are few, if any, precedents, it would be better for everyone concerned to admit that both going in and staying out involve a 'leap of faith'. But the Treasury persists in its misguided quest for comprehensive and copper-bottomed guarantees, extending the remit of the team charged with conducting the five tests to include three additional questions: To what extent did the introduction of euro notes and coins in the first two months of 2002 lead to opportunistic price hikes? How will joining the euro affect housing mortgage finance? And how does the SGP compare with Britain's own, self-imposed fiscal rules?

Convergence and flexibility

Of the original five tests, the most important are those concerning convergence and flexibility. The City of London remains Europe's leading financial centre and, indeed, has benefited from the new business generated by the euro, though its dominant position could begin to slip if Britain were to remain permanently outside it, especially if it were the *sole* EU member outside. Likewise, while there has not yet been a major exodus of foreign direct investment from Britain, the attitude of foreign investors depends critically on their belief that Britain will join the euro within the near future, and some American and Japanese companies have gone on record to say so. If this expectation were to be disappointed, many foreign firms with UK subsidiaries serving the whole European market are likely to relocate inside the euro-zone in order to protect their European sales from the risk of exchange rate fluctuations. Already, Britain, which used to attract more new foreign investment from outside the EU than any other Member State, has seen its share of the annual inflow fall since the launch of the euro. Finally, the last of the five tests, concerned with growth, stability and employment, is a compendium question, the answer to which depends on the answers to the other four.

Cyclical convergence is a commonsense requirement. Even the most ardent Europhile would accept that it was not met in 1997, when the UK economy was booming, while the main European economies were still in the doldrums. Since then, however, economic trajectories have moved closer together and, with one exception, the UK now satisfies all the so-called Maastricht convergence criteria: its inflation rate and long-term interest rates are about the same as those in the euro-zone; short-term interest rates are about one percentage point apart; the UK government's budget deficit is well below the permitted ceiling; and at less than 40% of GDP, gross government debt at the end of 2001 was the third lowest in Europe. The exception is the exchange rate. Under the terms of the Maastricht Treaty, first-wave entrants to the euro were required to keep their exchange rates 'within the normal margin of fluctuation of the ERM' for at least two years before joining. Nothing was said about subsequent entrants and, in any case, in 1993 the ERM margins were widened from ± 2.25 % of parity to ±15%. In fact, from early 2000 to late 2002, sterling was fairly *stable* against the euro, trading in the range €1.70 – 1.60 per pound or £0.59 – 0.62 per euro. The trouble is that even the bottom end of this range – equivalent to 3.13 Deutsche Marks – was above the level that proved unsustainable when sterling was in the ERM and has imposed a heavy competitive handicap on British industry. In recent months, however, the rate has dropped below €1.50 and could be brought down further to a sustainable level – perhaps around €1.40 per pound or £0.71 per euro – once the markets became convinced that Britain was set to join and a target entry rate had been agreed with the ECB.

The flexibility test turns on what problems the UK might face inside the euro area and what is meant by 'flexible response'. The main potential for trouble arises from what economists call an 'asymmetric shock': that is, an unforeseen change in the economic or political environment that affects the UK more than other countries in the euro area. Such problems do occur from to time: for example, the collapse of the Russian economy after the fall of communism made a large hole in Finland's export markets and caused widespread job losses; or again, the reunification of Germany in 1991 imposed a heavy fiscal burden on the West German economy, though in this case the 'shock' was the result of policy decisions taken by West German government, and the repercussions spread to other EU member states which, having pegged their currencies to the Deutsche Mark, were forced to follow suit when the Bundesbank raised German interest rates. If a country in the euro area were to encounter similar problems, it could be in difficulties, partly because it is no longer able to use the interest rate and exchange rate as tools of macroeconomic adjustment, and partly because the EU lacks the internal labour mobility and large central budget that a federal state such as the US can bring to the aid of regions in distress.

Recent experience suggests, however, that it may be possible to develop alternative adjustment capabilities. In several EU countries – mainly, but not only, the smaller ones – the prospect of monetary union in the 1990s had the unforeseen effect of reviving the practice of social partnership and policy negotiation that was widely thought to have been killed off by globalisation. Governments which anticipated difficulty in maintaining low inflation and a stable currency, while keeping their budget deficits under control, sought to engage their social partners in a multilateral process of negotiation and problem-solving aimed at strengthening their combined capacity for flexible response. In some cases, such as Denmark, the Netherlands and the Irish Republic, the range of participants extended beyond employers' associations and trade unions to include organizations representing disadvantaged groups such as the long-term unemployed, women and ethnic minorities which, in the past, were excluded from the corridors of power. The agenda of negotiation was similarly broad, starting on the familiar ground of wage bargaining, employment, taxation and social security, but branching out via policy linkages and spillovers into adjacent parts of the work-welfare complex such as childcare, education and training, housing, transport, health and social services. Of course, it may be that the UK as a whole is too big, too diverse and too deeply in thrall to the rule of the market to emulate these examples, but Scotland may be better placed, with its small population, relative cohesion, collectivist traditions and newly devolved government. To quote the conclusion of a recent report on Scottish independence: 'Scotland could join the ranks of small, activist democracies able to use their social integration to adapt quickly to change and maintain a degree of manoeuvre in an interdependent world.' [6] [7]

[6] See Murkens *et al.* (2002)

[7] The experience of social pacts in Europe during the 1990s is reviewed in Fajertag and Pochet (eds) (2000)

Fiscal and monetary policy in the euro-zone

What of the euro-zone's fiscal and monetary arrangements? Under the SGP, governments are required to keep their budgets 'close to balance' – not every single year, but on average over the course of the business cycle. No distinction is drawn between *current* public spending on items such as the wages of public employees or social security payments, and *capital* spending on fixed public assets such as roads and hospitals: the pact simply stipulates that any government whose overall budget deficit exceeds 3% of GDP can be ordered to take action to bring it below this ceiling or face a fine that could be as large as 0.5% of GDP. There is an escape clause in the case of a serious recession, but this is too tightly defined to be of much practical use: GDP has to fall by as much as 2% in one year – a rare occurrence. The European Commission is the overseer of the pact, but punitive measures require a two thirds majority in the Council of Ministers.

The original idea behind the pact was to prevent national governments from undermining the anti-inflationary work of the ECB by loosening fiscal policy. The danger is that the rules are too restrictive. In a recession, the fiscal straitjacket they impose may make things worse, forcing governments to cut public spending or raise taxes at the very time when they should be seeking to *stimulate* economic activity. But the danger should not be exaggerated. There have been very few periods since the Second World War when budget deficits in European countries have exceeded 3 per cent for longer than a year.[8] Moreover, fiscal policy is always constrained by the need to reassure financial markets that the government's stance is 'sound' (according to the conventions of the day) and it is quite specious to suggest that the UK would enjoy *more* freedom of action outside the SGP.

[8] See B. Eichengreen and C. Wyplosz, 'The Stability Pact: More than a Minor Nuisance?' in Begg (ed) (1998).

Certainly, Gordon Brown's 'golden rule' – that current public spending should, on average, be covered by tax receipts, with borrowing only for capital projects – has not so far proved *less* conservative than the SGP. Of course, this could well change over the next three years, given the UK government's plans to increase the share of GDP spent on key public services and the growing likelihood that the growth forecasts on which these plans were based will turn out to be too optimistic. In general, however, the conventional wisdom being what it is, announcing and following *some* set of rules is probably the best, and perhaps the only, way of maintaining investor confidence, though as times change the rules will need to change with them if governments are not to find themselves continuing to fight old wars just as new ones are breaking out.

The present conjuncture is a case in point. When the SGP was agreed in 1996, the thirty-years' war against inflation was still the top priority of economic policy, though even then the war was all but won. Now, however, with the end of the dotcom investment boom and the collapse of the world's stock markets, the principal threat facing the advanced capitalist countries is not inflation, but stagnation, with the price level *falling* year by year rather than rising. Indeed, in Japan over the past decade the threat of deflation has become a reality and, if the current global slowdown is not handled with care, the same could happen in North America and Europe. One predictable result of the slowdown is that budget deficits have started to rise as tax revenues fall and more is paid out in social security benefits to the unemployed. This is a benign development, for it helps to arrest the momentum of recession by shoring up aggregate spending. It has, however, caused several EU countries – including France, Germany and Portugal – to breach the 3% ceiling. In these circumstances, to insist on the letter of the SGP is to increase the risk of a generalised slump and so far EU finance ministers have wisely chosen to bend the rules in order to allow the built-in fiscal stabilisers to do their work, though not without being admonished for their pains by the President of the ECB and the EU

Finance Commissioner, who accused them of endangering the euro's credibility. This suggests that if the UK government were to press for a change in the rules, it might well find powerful allies. Of course, it has little influence as long as it remains outside the euro-zone, but fiscal reform could and should be included in the negotiations that would have to precede Britain's entry. One option would be to raise the permitted deficit ceiling and/or widen the range of exceptions – acknowledging, for example, that economic forecasting is a hazardous business, that the distinction between 'structural' and 'cyclical' budget deficits can only be confidently applied in retrospect and that all fiscal rules should be applied with discretion. Additional flexibility could be gained by adopting Gordon Brown's 'golden rule', incorporating the distinction between current and capital spending and accommodating governments which, like Britain's, have low levels of public debt, but urgently need to refurbish their public infrastructure. In a symbolic change of word order, the new regime might be called the 'Growth and Stability Pact'.

Complementary reforms are needed in the ECB, whose remit and procedures also bear the mark of neo-liberal dogma and need to be brought into line with best practice. Like the Bank of England, the ECB should be given a symmetrical inflation target, with a floor, as well as a ceiling, on the permissible rate of inflation; and like the US Federal Reserve Board, it should be obliged to take account of growth and employment prospects when setting interest rates. The Bank should also be made more accountable by publishing the minutes of its board meetings, voting records and all. More generally, its deliberations need to be embedded within an ongoing, EU-wide conversation about macroeconomic policy, involving not only the European Parliament and national finance ministries, but also employers, trade unions and the wider range of social interest groups which have a legitimate part to play in shaping public policy and are willing to share responsibility for economic management. This is desirable not just on democratic grounds, but in order to underpin a commitment to monetary ease by setting up a virtuous interaction between central bank and civil society. The greater the Bank's confidence that cheap money will not give rise to inflation, the less the risk that economic expansion will be terminated by monetary stringency, the better the outlook for investment, jobs and budgetary balances, the higher the Bank's public standing and the more willing the social partners to exercise restraint in pursuit of sectional claims, whether for higher wages, increased public spending, lower taxes or less regulation.

The political architecture of the EU is discussed more fully in the next section. To conclude the more narrowly focused argument of this section, it suffices to note that the euro is about passions and politics, not just a question of economics. For Britain's EU partners, EMU is the symbol and touchstone of its European allegiance. Only if and when Britain adopts the euro, will the ghost of perfidious Albion be exorcised. Conversely, only if and when the British people make a full commitment to the EU, will they finally accept that their 'destiny' lies in Europe, not in North America, or even in mid-Atlantic.

3

EU Enlargement and Reform

THE EU IS POISED on the brink of a major enlargement. When this is complete, the Union will stretch from Lappland to Limassol and from Tralee to Talinn. Three related issues are pressing: What further measures of economic and political integration, if any, are needed to buttress the single currency? How can the EU become a more cohesive and effective actor on the world stage? And how can the EU resolve its internal crisis of legitimacy?

The last of these, in particular, is critical for the future. By and large, until the early 1990s, the process of European integration was underpinned by a 'permissive consensus' which allowed political leaders to drive it forward without needing to make much effort to carry the public with them. If 'Eurocrats' were somewhat remote and unaccountable, this was a defect that could be tolerated in exchange for the benefits that integration was believed to confer: the preservation of peace and the promotion of prosperity throughout the continent. Over the past decade, however, this familiar story has become less reassuring – think, for example, of the wars that accompanied the break-up of Yugoslavia or the austerity that was imposed in the run-up to the single currency – and there has been a marked decline in popular support for the EU, with adverse shifts in opinion poll ratings, 'shock' results in national referenda and falling turnout rates in elections for the European Parliament. Worse still, successive national elections over the past two years have brought an upsurge of support for parties of the populist and xenophobic right whose litany of threats to the integrity of the 'nation' now includes – alongside asylum-seekers, migrant workers, foreign terrorists, international criminals, alien cultures and global capital – the EU's liberal, cosmopolitan elite. For the time being, these new variant forms of fascism remain on the margins of

European politics, but in certain conditions – for example, if the current economic slowdown were to degenerate into a full-scale global slump – they could penetrate the mainstream, blocking the enlargement of the EU and aggravating tensions within and between its member states.

Thus, the challenges facing the EU are as great as any in its history. Impending enlargement is forcing the pace of reform both in policy substance and in political structures; action is urgently required to avert recession and revive Europe's faltering growth; the emerging American Empire poses big questions about the role of the EU in global politics; and EU leaders need to find ways of restoring the faith of their own citizens in European ideals and institutions. For the sake of clarity or simply because it is impossible to discuss everything at once, these issues are often treated separately. They are, nevertheless, interconnected: the solutions offered in one area have implications for the others. By way of illustration, consider three specific cases: the reform of the EU budget and the Common Agricultural Policy (CAP), the problem of migrant workers and the Convention on the Future of Europe.

Budgetary reform, the CAP and the free movement of labour

EU expenditure is currently 1 per cent of European GDP and less than 4 per cent of the combined spending of central governments in its Member States. About half of it goes on the CAP, a further 30 per cent on regional aid, 15 per cent on the EU Social Fund and the rest on EU administration. A linchpin of the Franco-German axis around which the original EEC revolved, the CAP has since served to redistribute income from those Member States where agriculture has dwindled into insignificance to those where it still forms a sizeable fraction of the economy, including four relatively poor countries – Greece, Ireland, Portugal and Spain – and three much richer ones – Denmark, Finland and France. The states which have hitherto paid for this largesse – mainly Germany and the Netherlands – were reluctant to go on doing so even before the cost of agricultural subsidies and regional aid threatened to multiply with the accession of countries such as Poland, which is very poor and has lots of farmers. To lower tensions and gain time, the Commission proposed that newcomers should receive only 25% of the level of direct subsidy paid to existing EU farmers, rising to 100% only after ten years. Understandably, this left applicant states feeling aggrieved, but might have been acceptable as part of a wider reform package. In the autumn of 2002, however, the French government orchestrated a successful defence of the CAP in its traditional form and the Dutch and German governments, which had argued for the ending of farm production subsidies and the redirection of the money saved towards rural development, were forced to agree to delay any major reforms until 2006. Meanwhile, poor third-world countries, desperate to improve the lot of their own primary producers and boost their earnings of foreign exchange, have joined forces with major agricultural exporters such as Australia, Argentina and Brazil in pressing the EU to widen access to its markets by removing protection from European farmers. Even in a normal political climate, it would be difficult to strike a balance between these conflicting claims. Given the loss of public faith in the EU and the rise of the far right, it is much harder for mainstream politicians to deal generously with applicant countries, while at the same time keeping the EU budget under control, redistributing the burden of paying for it and replacing farm production subsidies by payments for environmental stewardship and rural development.

Another potentially explosive consequence of enlargement is the free movement of workers from the east. Even Greece, the poorest of the EU's existing member states, has a higher per capita income than Slovenia, the richest of the central European applicants, and whereas the ratio between the richest and poorest countries in the EU is currently about 2:1, after enlargement it will widen to 7:1. Levels of poverty, joblessness and all-round human misery are even higher in the countries of the former USSR and despite the efforts currently being made to tighten EU border controls, as the union's external frontier is extended it is likely to become more porous. Little wonder, then, if the previously secure and affluent populace of western Europe is fearful that enlargement will open the floodgates to a tide of immigration from the east, driving down wages, forcing up housing costs, overwhelming public services and provoking ethnic strife. From a long run perspective, such fears are groundless. The comparative and historical evidence shows unequivocally that immigrants, being generally young, energetic, adaptable and enterprising, help to raise general living standards, not drag them down. Moreover, given that birth rates throughout Western Europe have fallen to well below the population–replacing rate of 2.1 children per woman, while life expectancy continues to rise, the chances are that over the next fifty years immigrants will be needed to offset labour shortages and support ageing populations, though in what numbers no one knows, since economic, as well as demographic, factors are involved. In the long run, however, we are all dead and, in the meantime, the anxieties of domestic voters must be assuaged, the rhetoric of right-wing populists resisted, the movement of migrant workers managed, and the development of poor countries assisted, not least in order to ensure that their human resources are employed where they are needed most.

The Convention on the Future of Europe

The questions facing Convention on the Future of Europe are more elevated, but no less emotive. Should the EU have a constitution and, if so, what kind: one incorporating lofty ethical principles like that of the US, a systematic legal code on the Napoleonic model, or a pragmatic consolidation of existing EU treaties, as advocated by the UK? How should the Europe's governing institutions be reformed? And what is the appropriate division of powers and responsibilities between supranational agencies, national governments and 'sub-member state administrations', as devolved government is delicately, if inelegantly, known in EU jargon? All these issues arouse fierce passions and controversy, much of it conducted and reported in grandiose and facile terms. By analogy with the Philadelphia Convention of 1787 which drew up the constitution of the USA, it is often suggested that the main line of division runs between 'federalists' who favour a strong, supranational tier of government leading ultimately to a 'United States of Europe', and 'minimalists' who want to limit the pooling of sovereignty to the least that is required to maintain a 'United Europe of States'. Of course, in an evolving union of semi-sovereign nation-states, which have agreed to co-operate for certain restricted but important purposes, yet remain jealous of their ancient and hard-won prerogatives, disputes about ultimate goals and who should do what are endemic. There are, nevertheless, other significant issues that do not fall into this category: notably, how to overcome Europe's 'democratic deficit', whatever the balance of authority and power between different levels of government.

What, for example, should be done to clarify the respective roles of the EU's two most powerful institutions, the Commission and the Council? Historically, the Commission has served as a supranational bureaucracy, subordinate to the Council and responsible for technical tasks such as drafting legislation and monitoring compliance; but it has also been the dynamo of the European project, keeping alive the goal of 'ever closer union', even in times of stalemate and paralysis, and promoting ambitious initiatives such as the Single Market programme in the 1980s and EMU in the 1990s. The Council too has played a dual role, with ministers striving simultaneously to defend national interests, as interpreted at any given time by the governments they represent, and to work for the greater good of 'Europe'. And to compound these ambiguities, EU policy-making tends to proceed by bargaining, coalition-building and consensus, amidst multiple networks of lobbies and interest-groups, some of which are decidedly more equal than others. A worse design for promoting such classic democratic ideals as transparency, accountability, accessibility and fairness would be hard to imagine.

Various ideas for streamlining EU governance have been proposed. One is to end the cumbersome practice of rotating the Presidency of the Council among member states every six months and, instead of a President of the Commission appointed by the elected heads of government, to have a directly elected EU President who would chair Council meetings (held at more frequent intervals) expedite Council business in-between meetings and represent the EU on the world stage. The new President might perhaps be flanked by three deputies or high representatives, who would preside over the three principal ministerial Councils: economics and finance, defence and foreign affairs, and justice and home affairs. To counterbalance the resulting accretion of coherence and power at the apex of the EU, the secrecy that currently surrounds the work of the Council should be swept away and all legislation emanating from it should require the approval of the European Parliament.

There is much to be said for this scheme, but it is opposed by the larger Member States, who see a directly elected EU Presidency as a threat to their power and legitimacy. An alternative proposal, jointly devised by France and Germany and backed by the other big states, including the UK, is for the EU to have two Presidents serving concurrent, five-year terms: one elected by MEPs to head the Commission, and the other chosen by elected heads of government to preside over the Council. This idea has been condemned by 'federalists' as a recipe for conflict and confusion, and finds little favour with the smaller states, which fear that it would allow the bigger countries to stitch up deals between themselves and impose them on the rest.[9]

It makes little sense, however, to ponder the merits of rival reform proposals without first asking: What is the EU for? Consider the following analogy. Imagine that a community of once warring neighbours issues invitations for the design of a new

---

[9] The current composition, powers and functions of the EU's key policy-making institutions are summarised in Appendix 2.

building in which to transact their communal business. The neighbours used to be proudly independent and their dealings with each other were conducted largely on the basis of (domestic) self-interest, but they have recently removed the barriers that formerly divided them and, while retaining control over internal matters that do not concern outsiders, have agreed to joint decision-making in areas where they judge that they have more to gain by acting together than by staying apart, not least in their dealings with the rest of the world. An architect who is concerned, above all, to preserve and, if possible, enhance the degree of democracy that used to prevail in the old days of segregated autonomy and mutual rivalry, submits a multi-storey, open-plan design, providing for easy access from one level to the next, see-through internal walls and ceilings so that every household (or its representatives) can at all times keep an eye on what the others are doing, and rapid-transit corridors connecting their previously separate residences.

Now, the aims of this joint venture are admirable. So are the ideals of the architect. But in a context where memories of old wars are fading and new threats to peace and prosperity are looming, an appeal to purely *instrumental* values such as accessibility, transparency, speed and efficiency is not enough to revive enthusiasm for the project among households who may be more familiar with their neighbours than they used to be, but are too busy earning a living, consuming commodities and raising children – in that order – to pay much attention to politics and, insofar as they do take an interest, are more concerned with domestic issues on the ground floor (or 'grass roots' as it would have been called in an earlier, agrarian age) than with what goes on above their heads, at the higher levels of community government. The only kind of design that has any chance of gaining their approval is one that appeals to their most cherished values, addresses their fears, reminds them of their history and gives them hope for the future.

The Convention is meeting in a void. Notwithstanding the 'Ode to Joy', the starry blue flag and the tears shed by central bankers at the launch of the euro, the EU does not inspire the patriotism that was once evoked by the idea of the nation, binding its members together even as it set them apart from outsiders. The nation as an imagined community may be in decline, but it has not been replaced by any wider, *supranational* focus of emotional loyalty and political action, though the process of European integration *has* given a boost to the renaissance of regions and small nations that were previously submerged within larger nation-states, providing them with sources of funding, channels of influence and models of development beyond their old boundaries and horizons. Demands for regional autonomy have gained added legitimacy from the principle of subsidiarity. Originally devised by the Catholic Church in order to protect faith-based social services against encroachment by the secular state and pressed into service by national governments anxious to limit the transfer of powers to the EU, the principle establishes a presumption that political decisions should be taken as close as possible to those whom they affect unless it can be shown that the objectives sought would be more effectively achieved by action at a higher level of government. Of course, separatist movements are not inherently virtuous. Italy's Northern League, for example, represents a noxious, sub-Thatcherite brew of xenophobia and petit-bourgeois prejudice. Nor has the EU been much help in resolving sectarian conflict in Northern Ireland or the war of secession in the Basque country. Nevertheless, a multi-tiered 'Europe of the regions' is a desirable goal and progress towards it would help to revitalise democratic politics generally and restore faith in the EU itself.

At present, however, except for the occasional referendum, EU politics remains an elite business. Multinational party groupings in the European Parliament are cosmopolitan, but rootless, and the link between parliamentary representation and executive power, the fulcrum of democracy in the nation-state, is missing from the institutions of the EU. There is, in short, no pan-European *demos* and no corresponding European public realm in which collective choices are defined and debated, public opinion moulded and mobilised, political leadership tried and tested and public policies decided and implemented.

This is why the analogy with the birth of the USA is flawed.[10] The Philadelphia Convention was held in the triumphal aftermath of a revolutionary war against colonial rule. Before the war, the American colonies had enjoyed wide *de facto* autonomy, but had all been subject to the British Crown and, to that extent, had all belonged to a common polity. Hence, among the delegates to the Convention there was a tacit agreement that functions previously reserved to the British Crown would be inherited by the new federal government. Moreover, whereas the EU has been built from the top down, American political development proceeded from the bottom up. Habituated to self-government, New Englanders first created townships, then state governments and, finally, a federal state. Their fledgling democracy was also sustained by shared moral beliefs. The early American settlers embraced a liberal version of Christianity which prescribed 'equal liberty' and stressed the importance of conscience and voluntary assent rather than authority and obedience. Thus, having adopted a Constitution that sanctified the private sphere of choice and set clear limits to the legitimate scope of state activity, denizens of the 'land of the free' could live as 'one nation under God'. A common language was a further unifying factor, though its full value only became apparent in the late nineteenth and early twentieth centuries when the US assimilated millions of immigrants from eastern and southern Europe who did not share the religion and mores of the original settlers or their experience of self-government and commitment to personal freedom. For some groups, of course, the famous 'melting pot' was more of a consuming fire. Vanquished Native Americans and imported African slaves remained excluded from white society, while the attempted secession of the southern states was only resolved by

---

[10] This paragraph draws heavily on Siedentop (2000).

bloody force of arms. But if the experience of genocide, slavery and civil war left America permanently divided and disfigured, the transforming power of myth and story turned even the dark side of its past to account in the making of the nation.

It does not, however, follow that the European project is doomed. To repeat: the history of European integration is not a re-run of the history of the nation-state, nor, as things stand, does a United States of Europe look remotely feasible, even if it were desirable. But what, in positive terms, is the EU for? As we have seen, there are two stock answers: one relies on outworn platitudes; the other invokes purely functional qualities which are valued not for their own sake, but because they serve as means to ulterior ends, yet fails to spell out what these ends might be. To find a better answer, we must pursue the comparison between Europe and America further in order to identify what is distinctive about the societies that developed in the old world. Then we need to decide which features of European civilisation are still worth defending, whether they still strike a chord in the hearts of Europe's citizens and how they can best be preserved in the face of the forces and threats ranged against them.

4

Europe versus America:
A Tale of Two Capitalisms

OVER THE PAST few years, the EU has frequently clashed with the US government. Clearly, some of the blame lies with the Bush administration which, particularly since 9/11 – or 11/9 as Europeans would say – has been more arrogant and aggressive in its dealings with other countries, even friendly ones, than any of its predecessors in living memory. But there is more to what is happening than this. As Will Hutton (2002) argues, in his book, *The World We're In*, recent tensions between Europe and America spring from differences of history and culture and have far-reaching implications for the shape of the emergent world order.

In one sense, Hutton's title is misleading. What he offers is not a panoramic survey, but a focused comparison between two very different kinds of capitalism: the various forms of social capitalism that have evolved in Western Europe and the free market individualism that was born in the USA. These two models, he argues, embody sharply contrasting conceptions of property rights, citizenship and the public realm. In Europe, where capitalism developed out of the seedbed of feudalism under the tutelary gaze of a state church that claimed moral and spiritual authority over the whole of Christendom, property-ownership came to be understood as a form of stewardship, exercised on behalf of society as a whole. The privileges it conferred – to decide how resources are used, to direct the process of production and to receive a portion of the fruits – were never absolute, but always qualified by corresponding social obligations, summed up in the precept 'Noblesse oblige', which in today's world might be taken as meaning that *all* sources of social advantage – not just inherited land and social rank, but money, office, talents and skills – confer responsibilities on those who possess them.

In various guises, this root idea was preserved by all the main European political traditions: liberalism, social democracy, communism, Christian democracy, one-nation conservatism and even fascism. It came near to being repudiated in the nineteenth century by English political economists, precursors of today's neo-liberals, who proclaimed the virtues of the unfettered market and prescribed a minimalist role for the state. But laissez-faire was an aberration from the European norm and even in Britain its heyday was brief and its dominance less than total. The reforming zeal of Victorian liberalism is hard to square with the image of society as a collection of atomistic, self-interested individuals, whose interactions are regulated by 'natural' economic law. Likewise, the luminaries of British liberalism in the twentieth century – Lloyd-George, Hobson, Beveridge and Keynes – were all confirmed collectivists who insisted that far from curtailing personal freedom, policies such as tax-financed social security, state education, town planning and macroeconomic management were pre-requisites of it. Elsewhere in Europe, from Gambetta to De Gaulle, from Bismarck to Adenauer, and from Giolitti to De Gasperi, the issue was not *whether* the state should intervene to regulate the functioning of the market, but *what kind of* collectivism was to prevail in the struggle for mastery of the nation's destiny.

In the course of this struggle, the idea that citizenship entails significant *social* rights and duties came to be more or less taken for granted. Once fascism was defeated and liberal democracy restored to Western Europe, even the enemies of socialism came to accept that it was not enough for all (national) citizens to enjoy equality before the law, civil liberties and the right to vote in elections for government. In societies where capitalism is the dominant mode of production and competitive market forces govern the allocation of resources and rewards, there are bound to be winners and losers, and in the absence of countervailing social arrangements that are not themselves subject to the logic of the market, not only will some people be permanently disadvantaged, but the resulting inequalities in life-chances are liable to harden into permanent social divisions, weakening social cohesion and undermining political stability. The problem is to set limits to the operation of the market, without compromising civil and political freedom. Or to rephrase this question in positive terms: what do people need if they are to become and remain autonomous and responsible agents, capable of thinking for themselves, making their own choices and decisions and shaping their lives in accordance with their deepest values and beliefs?

Social citizenship and the democratic state

The solution, in theory, is to distinguish between two kinds of need-satisfying facilities: those to which people *must* have access if they to acquire and retain the requisite capabilities; and those which people should be free to choose for themselves. Standard examples of the former kind, 'primary goods'[11] as they are often known, are adequate health and education, housing and income security, emotional security in childhood and a position or role in society role that gives one a sense of self-respect. Subject to certain safeguards, the production and distribution of 'secondary goods' should be left to private initiative and discretion, whether within a market or non-market framework. But access to primary

[11] This term has the advantage of being short and hallowed by usage among (Anglo-American) political philosophers, but the disadvantage of being associated in English with 'merchandise' or 'commodities', which is perhaps not altogether surprising in societies where money will buy almost anything. It is used here to refer to every kind of material or cultural product that serves to satisfy human wants and/or needs, regardless of any other characteristics the product might have, such as how it is produced, whether its producers are paid, whether it is sold on a market, whether – once it exists – people can be excluded from consuming or using it, whether its consumption or use by one person diminishes the amount available for others or, for better or worse, affects them in some other way, and whether it is generally regarded as a 'good thing' or a 'bad thing'.

goods must be guaranteed by the state as an entitlement of citizenship. That is the only way to ensure that all citizens can participate effectively in the various spheres of social life – whether as employees, consumers and savers; as taxpayers, service-users and voters; as parents, partners and friends; or, finally, as members of the countless interest groups and voluntary associations that help to keep civil society going.

Which goods are primary; what standards are 'adequate'; whether primary goods should both financed and *produced* by the state; how public services should be organised; who should bear the cost; and how far the public sector *can* be insulated from the market, were questions that became the staples of political debate. The answers varied from country to country, depending on the peculiarities of national history and the balance of political forces, and often the consequences were disappointing or gave rise to new problems that were not foreseen when welfare states were still in their infancy. But if the ideal of social citizenship proved ambiguous and elusive as soon as it was translated into a viable working model, much the same could be said of attempts to establish a democratic system of government. After all, even in a secure, unitary state where there are no disputes over external borders or internal jurisdictions, where parliamentary institutions are strong and where popular commitment to peaceful forms of political activity runs deep, the democratic agenda would be far from exhausted: indeed, some of the most difficult puzzles and problems would remain unsolved. 'Universal suffrage', for example, is normally taken to mean that all legally resident adults have the right to vote. But how does anyone become a legal resident and what about the interests of children? Or again, which of the various possible voting systems offers the best attainable compromise among competing *desiderata*: reasonably compact electoral districts with roughly equal numbers of voters and impartially drawn boundaries, high turnout rates, no 'wasted' votes, proportionality between votes cast and seats won, close links between local constituencies and elected representatives, clear-cut electoral verdicts and stable government?[12] How should we set about equipping and encouraging citizens to participate in public affairs? And most formidable of all: what can be done to create a level political playing field, free from the distortions produced by unequal resources, superior organisation, vested interest and structural bias? The republic of heaven may never be built on earth, but that is no reason to stop trying to improve the state we are in. 'Fail again', urged Samuel Beckett, 'Fail better!'

In any case, for all the flaws of actually existing welfare states, the *idea* of collective responsibility for assuring minimum standards of employment, health care, income and the rest, has gained a hold in people's values and beliefs which even twenty years of retrenchment and restructuring have done little to shake. Voters may be dissatisfied with public services and may approve, or be persuaded to accept, proposals for reform, but in the world of welfare-capitalism advocates of capitalism without welfare still have a hard row to hoe. Levels of support for existing welfare states vary, being highest in 'big spenders' such as Sweden and France, and lowest in 'low spenders' such as the USA and Australia, but broadly similar patterns emerge everywhere. Retirement pensions, health care/insurance and child/family allowances – the most extensive and expensive elements of state provision – are the most popular; social assistance for minorities who are perceived as 'scroungers' is the least popular, though even in this case there is little support for removing the social safety-net altogether.[13]

Admittedly, the welfare state long ago lost its lustre as a symbol of collective promise, just as the high point of democratic advance was reached around the middle of the twentieth century. Since this time, though democracy has spread to countries that were previously under military or one-party rule, there has been a general decline both in political involvement and in the power

---

[12] Any self-respecting democracy, regardless of its voting system, should also have fixed-term parliaments.

[13] Pierson (1998) pp159-61 provides a concise review of the historical and comparative evidence on public attitudes to the welfare state.

of popular movements to secure reforms *within* each state, whether because of overt opposition by business interests, because national policy options are limited by structural constraints or because the movements themselves are fragmented, and can no longer extract concessions from their rulers by invoking the 'spectre' of communism. Nevertheless, while the arc of social and political development in the twentieth century followed a similar course on both sides of the Atlantic, in most of Western Europe, it attained a higher peak and, though subsequently falling, remained at a higher level than it did in the USA.[14]

American capitalism and the conservative revolution

From its origins, the US has been the world's most thoroughly bourgeois society. Settlers in a land of opportunity with no feudal past, Americans have devoted their lives to self-betterment and, except in periods of desperate social crisis, have spurned collectivist politics, seeing no legitimate role for the state except as policeman, incarcerator and warrior. Accordingly, property in the US is relatively unencumbered by social responsibility; the social dimension of citizenship is stunted and fragile; and the public realm is deformed by the power of money, the shallowness of the media and the decline in civic participation. To be sure, from the New Deal of the 1930s to the Great Society programme of the 1960s, American liberalism gained the upper hand and successive Democratic administrations set about managing and regulating the economy, establishing the rudiments of a welfare state and ending racial oppression. But from the early 1970s onwards, these advances were steadily eroded as the conservative right, favoured by the shift of capital and population from rust-belt to sun-belt and by the unravelling of the old Democratic coalition loosely knit from northern trade unions, southern

---

[14] Crouch (2000) uses the image of a parabola to describe the progress and regress of democracy in the advanced capitalist states during the twentieth century.

whites, enfranchised blacks, rural smallholders and the urban intelligentsia, proceeded to assemble its own hegemonic coalition, challenging the assumptions of the post-war consensus, securing the support of big business and basing its popular appeal on a potent blend of anti-statist individualism, 'America-first' militarism, white backlash racism and crusading moral authoritarianism. Unrestrained by significant collective resistance – whether based in social institutions, like the NHS, in popular movements, like trade unions, or in ideological traditions, like socialism and Christian democracy – the conservative worldview swept all before it, forcing the Democrats to reposition themselves and, outside the US, capturing strongholds both in international agencies such as the IMF, the World Bank and the OECD, and in other states, particularly in the English-speaking world.

The differences between the European and American models of capitalism would matter less if the claims made for the latter were true: for example, that US companies are more successful than their European counterparts or that the US record in generating jobs or promoting social mobility is unmatched. In fact, such claims are not borne out by the evidence. Take employment and unemployment, for example. According to the conventional wisdom, 'Europe' is worse than the US at creating new jobs and reducing joblessness because its labour markets are 'sclerotic' and need to be made more flexible. When it was first propounded by the OECD (1994), this argument seemed superficially plausible, but it has since been overtaken by events. From the early 1990s onwards, employment rates rose and unemployment rates fell in Denmark, Ireland, the Netherlands, Sweden and the UK. (Unemployment remained low throughout the 1980s and 1990s in 'forgotten' Austria and Portugal and, outside the EU, in Norway and Switzerland). Among the small open economies of Western Europe, only Belgium, Finland and Greece have continued to experience high unemployment. Among the large economies, unemployment remained high everywhere except the UK, but some improvement was achieved in France and

Spain, and although Germany has had high unemployment since the early 1990s, it is unclear how far this is due to 'structural rigidities' and how far to the continuing impact of re-unification. Certainly, German unemployment contains a strong regional component, the stark contrast between east and west paralleling the persistent north-south divide in Italy.[15] Meanwhile, across the Atlantic, the collapse of the dotcom boom has not only thrown the US 'jobs machine' into reverse, but has highlighted the weaknesses of an economic model based on deregulation, shareholder value and flexible markets: on the one hand, chronic job insecurity, excessive working hours and grotesque social inequality; on the other, corporate myopia, irrational exuberance and the risk of a major depression.[16]

[15] This summary of recent trends in European employment and unemployment draws on the excellent survey provided by Andersen, JG and Halvorsen, K (2002) 'Unemployment, welfare policies and citizenship: different paths in Western Europe', in Andersen and Jensen (eds) (2002) pp 107-129.

[16] A statistical summary of the employment and unemployment records of the world's leading economies is presented in Appendix 1, Tables 1.3 and 1.4.

5

Social Capitalism and Global Politics

IT MIGHT BE ARGUED that although the differences between the two kinds of capitalism are real enough, the European model will be unable to hold out much longer against pressures to conform with the American way, for these are no longer confined to the battle of ideas and political campaigning, but have now become built into the institutions of the global economy. Consider the challenges facing Europe's welfare states. Even if the degree of global economic integration were no greater now than it was thirty years ago, governments would still have had to respond to a variety of pressures for change: from ageing populations, rising health costs, deindustrialisation, changing gender roles and the growing diversity of family and household forms; from the polarisation of life-chances and the changing profile of poverty; from the eclipse of the labour movement and the increased assertiveness of previously marginalised social groups such as ethnic minorities, gays and lesbians and disabled people; and from the decay of public confidence in the capacity of governments to solve social problems, the culture of consumerism and the emergence of a 'mixed economy of welfare'. As it is, external constraints bind far more tightly than in the past. Financial deregulation has curtailed the ability of national governments to pursue full (or fuller) employment. The ease with which transnational companies can shift profits, production and investment across national borders risks provoking tax competition among governments anxious to secure their favours, lowering the threshold of tax tolerance, squeezing public expenditure and damaging the framework of social solidarity. Furthermore increased dependence on foreign trade coupled with intensified international competition may drive some states into lowering standards of employment and social protection in a bid to save domestic jobs or steal a march on their rivals, putting pressure on others to follow suit and raising the spectre of a 'race to the bottom'.

Social pacts

It is, however, important to distinguish between the *logic* of globalisation and what has actually happened. Despite the undoubted shrinkage of national policy autonomy since the 'golden age' of the welfare state, some European governments have nevertheless managed to combine high levels of welfare spending with high rates of economic growth and falling unemployment: Denmark and the Netherlands are notable examples.[17] More generally, while globalisation inhibits welfare *spending*, national governments retain control over the *design* of welfare policy. Hence, given that untrammeled market freedom produces social dislocation, there is still a role for purposive public action to secure an acceptable balance between the interests of employers in not being over-regulated and overtaxed, the interests of employees in not being exploited and insecure, and the interests of non-employees in not being humiliated, poverty-stricken or excluded. Contrary to neo-liberal dogma, social protection need not destroy jobs or create rigidities. Thus, high levels of unionisation and collective bargaining coverage can be reconciled with high employment and low inflation provided wage bargaining is coordinated and trade unions do not become bastions of privilege. Similarly, generous unemployment benefits are perfectly compatible with low unemployment rates provided the demand for labour remains buoyant and active steps are taken to help jobless workers into employment. In addition some restrictions on the freedom of employers to hire and fire – the *external* dimension of labour market flexibility – are necessary if management and workers are to trust each other enough to agree on changes in working practices and effort standards – the *internal* dimension of flexibility.

[17] See Hirst and Thompson (1999) for a discussion of these cases.

Rhodes (2001) commends what he calls 'competitive corporatist' social pacts as a way of reconciling international market pressures with national social solidarity. The most advanced and enduring examples are the rolling agreements that underpinned the Dutch and Irish 'economic miracles' from the late 1980s onwards, but more limited pacts were concluded in Italy, Portugal and Spain during the 1990s. It is also worth noting the revival of corporatist negotiation in the Scandinavian countries and the continuing reluctance of German employers to give up the benefits they derive from *Mitbestimmung* or co-determination. Certainly, budgetary constraints have checked the growth of welfare spending everywhere and welfare states are being reshaped in response to common pressures, but there is no sign of transnational convergence in the scale or design of welfare provision. Nor is there any evidence that intensified competition has set in motion a downward spiral in standards of social protection. In short, national economies have not been wholly absorbed into the new global order, governments have not been totally incapacitated and the welfare state is not withering away.

Nevertheless, there are no grounds for complacency. The European social model – in reality, a mosaic of models with strong family resemblances – continues to be attacked by free marketeers both in the us and in Europe, and it would be unwise to put national social pacts under too much stress, particularly as the EU expands eastwards to include countries where standards of social protection are appreciably lower. Suppose the current economic slowdown continues, giving rise to recurrent budget deficits and sharpening commercial rivalry. Against this background, *generalised* reliance on 'competitive corporatism' could become counter-productive. If every member of an enlarged euro-zone is striving to keep ahead of the game, with no supranational rules to keep competition within bounds, each may end up having to work harder to stay in the same place and, since currency devaluation is no longer an option, countries that fall behind may be tempted to skimp on social standards, holding back their more progressive neighbours and creating an atmosphere of mutual mistrust.

So far 'social dumping' – deliberately lowering employment standards and social entitlements in a bid to cut costs, reduce domestic import penetration, gain a larger share of world export markets or attract footloose foreign investment – has been more of threat than a reality. But that is no reason not to take it seriously, particularly when building defences against it now offers important benefits at negligible cost in terms of resources expended or options foreclosed. As Mishra (1999) argues, standards of social protection should not be used as weapons in a competitive game, but must be part of the rules of the game. A precautionary, but conspicuous demonstration of commitment to this principle would reassure people that welfare reform was not a euphemism for welfare retrenchment and make it easier to negotiate social pacts, as well as helping to keep xenophobic and protectionist sentiment at bay.

Graduated welfare benchmarking

The problem is how to achieve this result. In certain areas of public policy the EU has succeeded in harmonising national regulations – health and industrial safety, environmental risks and consumer protection. But in the sphere of social protection and employment relations, the conflicts of interest are too intense to be settled within the EU's existing institutions, especially when times are hard. The chief obstacles stem from disparities of economic development and differences of policy regime. Rich countries or those with generous social standards are reluctant to scale down their workers' entitlements to benefits such as sick pay, annual holidays or parental leave. But poor EU countries, where output per worker is low, need to keep their wage and non-wage labour costs low as well if they are to compete in the internal market. Thus, unless the richer countries are willing to help them out, they cannot afford to agree to harmonisation through levelling up. But inter-state redistribution is not a popular cause at the best of times: recall the wrangling mentioned earlier over the reform of the CAP. Attempts to create an EU-wide social framework have also been bedevilled by ideological disputes about the legitimate scope of social policy, and by the reluctance of national governments to cede control over core welfare functions to the EU, for this is one of the few areas where national autonomy remains largely intact and its loss would gravely weaken their standing and power.

These obstacles, however, are not insuperable. One possibility, originally suggested by Scharpf (1997) and taken up by Mishra (1999), is to introduce a system of graduated welfare benchmarking, whereby national governments undertake to observe specified minimum social standards that become steadily more demanding as countries become more developed. For most purposes, national per capita income can be taken as a rough index of economic development, but in some cases other indicators such as national average earnings might be more suitable. Thus, richer countries would accept higher minimum standards than poor ones, but as the latter grew richer, their minimum standards would rise.

To see how such a system might work, consider the introduction of an EU-wide minimum wage agreement. Member States would first commit themselves to the *principle* of a statutory minimum wage, with provision, if necessary, for separate youth and adult rates. Then, instead of attempting the impossible task of setting a floor to wages throughout the EU at a uniform *absolute* level, they would agree not to let their own national minimum wage scales fall below some specified *proportion* of national average earnings. The precise position of the benchmark ratio would be a matter for negotiation. Clearly, the closer it lay to the lowest ratio actually prevailing in any member state, the easier it would be to reach agreement, for in that limiting case no country would have to raise its minimum wage: the club would merely be agreeing to build a firebreak at a point determined by its least generous member. But even an ultra-conservative commitment to the principle, 'Thus low and no lower', would have some value as a safeguard against social dumping, as well as drawing attention to existing inter-state disparities in relative minimum wages. And it should be possible to do better than this: the benchmark could, for example, be pitched *below* the ratio of minimum wages to average earnings prevailing in most states, but *above* the ratio permitted by a minority of laggards. The latter would agree to raise their standards on a phased, step-by-step basis, with provision for extending the timetable should they encounter an unforeseen rise in unemployment during the transition period.

Evidently, a similar approach could be applied to any social standard which admits of some form of measurement, if not directly, then by proxy, and if not on a cardinal scale where equal distances denote equal quantities, then at least on an ordinal scale which allows points to be ranked as higher or lower. Suitable cases include social security benefit scales and aggregate social expenditure (measured according to some agreed definition) as a proportion of GDP. The approach could also be extended to environmental standards, with governments agreeing to benchmarks for, say, air quality or waste recycling, which become progressively more exacting as countries become more affluent. Of course, one should not make a fetish of numbers or assume that everything has a price: some of the best things in life, though not free, cannot be adequately quantified – think of the value of human life itself or the value of biodiversity. In general, what counts matters more than what can be counted. Nevertheless, for certain public purposes – awarding compensation to victims of crime, say, or evaluating measures for reducing road accidents – there really is no rational alternative to using measurements of some kind. International comparisons of social and environmental standards fall into this category.

Not that graduated benchmarking is simply another tool for the 'Brussels bureaucracy', though this is how the idea might be portrayed by national-chauvinist tabloids and neo-liberal ideologues. It is, as already pointed out, an essentially conservative device designed to set a floor under international competition, thereby reproducing on a transnational scale the kind of regulation that was introduced in all European countries from the mid-nineteenth century onwards in a bid to protect both workers as individuals and society as whole against the unwanted consequences of unfettered capitalism. The difference is that whereas nineteenth century legislation to limit working hours or provide compensation for industrial accidents eventually culminated in the formation of national welfare states, its twenty-first century EU equivalents would emerge within a multi-tiered system of government, in which, as we noted earlier, the role of supranational agencies is largely confined to the *edges* of social policy space: that is, to issues that were not previously dealt with at any level or where established arrangements have been unhinged by the process of economic integration. There is no need or demand for the EU to pursue ambitious and costly social programmes of its own. Rather, its key task is to provide a regulatory framework that will keep global market forces within bounds so that democratic choices are not pre-empted and national governments are better able to achieve whatever collective social goals their citizens are willing to vote and pay for.

Looked at in this way, graduated benchmarking offers some important advantages. It accords with the principle of subsidiarity and cuts with the grain of recent EU development: national authorities would retain responsibility for social provision and environmental stewardship, but would work within a negotiated supranational framework. Existing member states would be covered by a common set of regulations, without compromising either the ability of the rich countries to maintain standards superior to the benchmarks or the ability of the poor countries to compete in the internal market. Candidate members would face a less daunting task in qualifying for admission. Indeed, as Mishra (1999) suggests, once a system of variable social and environmental thresholds was established in the EU, there is no reason why it could not be extended to other OECD countries or, eventually, to every country in the world. For the rich, industrialised countries basic social standards might consist of universal schooling and health care, social security programmes designed to keep the incidence of household poverty as close as possible to zero, statutory minimum wage and working hours limits, activist employment policies and anti-discrimination laws, some combination of in-kind services, income transfers and parental leave that gives mothers and fathers of children below school age a genuine choice between staying at home and participating in the labour market, and a parallel system of public support for severely disabled or frail elderly citizens and their carers. The corresponding requirements for the poorest countries of Asia and sub-Saharan Africa might amount to little more than primary health care, basic sanitation, safe drinking water and adequate nutrition.

Interestingly, in this connection, Mishra calls for a conceptual reorientation of social policy away from social *rights* to social *standards,* arguing that the language of rights is largely Western in origin and is alien to non-Western cultures, yet recognising that what is valuable about the concept of social citizenship is its concern with collective values such as social cohesion and social justice and its attachment to universal provision and balanced development as key aspirations. This is a useful corrective to a narrowly Eurocentric perspective and has some surprising implications. As things stand, on any reasonable set of benchmarks, the USA, the richest country in the world, would undoubtedly be found wanting with respect to health care and poverty. Imagine an ongoing global debate about proper standards of social protection, involving ordinary citizens as well as politicians and experts, and accompanied by the parallel evolution of a transnational social framework, confined initially to the EU, but gradually spreading to the rest of the world. In this context, it is not too fanciful to envisage a transnational coalition of rich and poor states making common cause with American trade unions and social movements to bring that country's backward welfare state into line with international norms.

Of course, the process of reaching multilateral agreements about what should be included in the baseline specification for each level of economic development, how each item should be measured and where the benchmark should be set, would be long and hard. But it would stimulate public debate about comparative welfare standards and the social dimension of citizenship both within each state and across the global village. Graduated benchmarking might also prompt parallel initiatives to deal with other global problems, from the reform of the international financial system and the conduct of transnational companies to the defence of human rights and the rehabilitation of collapsed states. In all these cases, the EU could galvanise a wider multilateral effort to socialise global capitalism, just as the rise of national parliamentary democracy hastened the demise of laisser-faire capitalism during the first half of the twentieth century and helped to bring about the international and national policy settlements that followed the Second World War.

As soon as the first benchmark was in place, however limited its scope and coverage, public concern about the social and environmental impact of economic development would acquire an institutional presence which, in the course of time, could be extended to other issues and states. Is it necessary to add that, to this end, all available international channels of communication and influence should be used: informal networks of activists, alliances of NGOs, periodic global summits and regular meetings of bodies such as the IMF, the WTO and UNESCO? 'Global resisters' who dismiss any prospect of reforming the institutions of global capitalism by working to change their founding statutes, leading personnel or ruling ideas are just as mistaken as their 'revolutionary' predecessors in the early twentieth century who ruled out participation in 'bourgeois' national parliaments as a distraction from extra-parliamentary politics. In both cases, the choice posed is a false one: the struggle to bring capitalism under social control had and still has many fronts, both at home and abroad.

The EU *as a global actor*

The EU is well placed to play a leading role in reshaping the global order. First, although the electoral and social coalitions that built and defended national welfare states are now in decline, for the time being their legacy survives in a complex of institutions, norms and practices that either never took root or became less deeply entrenched on the other side of the Atlantic: trade unions, collective bargaining, social citizenship, social partnership and the pursuit of the public good. In particular, as we have seen, the core institutions of the welfare state retain widespread popular support in all Member States. Similarly, despite endless propaganda extolling the superior 'efficiency' and 'dynamism' of the market, the public is far from convinced that industries and services which traditionally, and with good reason, have been 'close to the state' – water and energy supplies, transport facilities and postal and telecommunications systems – should be owned and run for profit by anonymous global corporations.

Second, while no one should underestimate the power of transnational companies, they are not invincible, and in the ongoing contest between the popular will and corporate might – an increasingly unequal contest on the terrain of the nation-state – the EU can bring to bear weapons that as yet have not been used. The euro-zone already represents about one sixth of world GDP, a share only slightly less than that of the US. If and when the UK joins, the economic weight of the two blocs will be roughly equal. As Hutton (2002, p. 364) notes, Europe would then have '… a world currency – the only conceivable challenger to the dollar, with all that implies, including the option of running its economy on more expansionary lines and a monetary umbrella under which it can insist that European regulations and approaches are complied with. Just as financial institutions and transnational companies comply with American rules to win the benefits of a New York listing and trading in the US, so the EU can play the same card.' The EU can, for example, simply refuse to enforce commercial contracts denominated in euros unless the companies concerned observe European standards in fields such as company law, accounting conventions, workplace consultation and environmental protection. The euro offers similar leverage in international politics. EU contributions to the IMF now exceed the dollar contributions made by the US: while the US has 17.78% of the votes, the EU has some 28% if it chooses to vote as a bloc (around 23% for the euro countries, plus Britain with 4.98%). So if the EU puts forward proposals for international financial reform, it can expect to be taken seriously.

Third, the EU has a wealth of experience in resolving or coping with the standard problems of multi-tiered government: notably, the tendency for the question, 'What is to be done?' to get entangled with the question, 'Who is to do it?' (Lenin famously reduced politics to the question: 'Who whom?' The issue posed by the EU is: 'Who what?') There is probably no perfect solution to this problem, but in a world of interacting states it has to be faced and because the EU has always been more than a mere confederation, but has stopped short of becoming a federal state, it offers a novel and flexible form of transnational partnership that has attracted interest in other parts of the world, such as Southern Africa, Latin America and South East Asia, where the practice of inter-governmental collaboration is only just beginning. At the very least, membership of the EU has helped to prevent Europe's big states from going to war with each other, engaging in mutually ruinous commercial rivalry or pursuing the delusion of national isolation. It has also protected their smaller neighbours from being bullied and coerced.

Finally, as a major trading bloc with extensive commercial, diplomatic and interpersonal connections in Eastern Europe, the Middle East and former colonies and dominions throughout the world, the EU could rally a powerful international coalition behind the cause of global reform, given the political will to mount a challenge to the present global order. This is the nub. Are European governments willing, or can they be persuaded, to break with neo-liberal fundamentalism and challenge American hegemony? Drawing on their shared traditions, collective clout, unique experience and external ties, are they ready to apply themselves to the task of building a better world order, one which promotes economic development in poor countries without undermining social standards in rich ones; which halts and reverses the despoliation of planet; and which supports the efforts of individual states to roll back the sway of the market and rebuild the structures of citizenship, if that is what their citizens desire?

Bibliography

Andersen, JG and Jensen, PH (eds.) (2002) *Changing Labour Markets, Welfare Policies and Citizenship* (Bristol: The Policy Press).

Begg, D (ed.) (1998) EMU *Prospects and Challenges* (Oxford: Oxford University Press).

Crouch, C (2000) *Coping with Post-Democracy* (London: The Fabian Society).

Dryden, S (1995) *Trade Warriors:* USTR *and the American Crusade for Free Trade* (Oxford: Oxford University Press).

Fajertag, G and Pochet, P (eds.) (2000) *Social Pacts in Europe: New Dynamics* (Brussels: European Trade Union Institute/ Observatoire Social Europeen).

Hirst, P and Thompson, G (1999) (2nd ed.) *Globalisation in Question* (Cambridge: Polity Press).

Hutton, W (2002) *The World We're In* (London: Little, Brown).

Mishra, R (1999) *Globalisation and the Welfare State* (Cheltenham, UK: Edward Elgar).

Murkens, J with Jones, P and Keating, M (2002) *Scottish Independence: A Practical Guide* (Edinburgh: Edinburgh University Press).

OECD (1994) *The* OECD *Jobs Study* (Paris: OECD).

Pierson, C (1998) (2nd ed.) *Beyond the Welfare State* (Cambridge: Polity Press).

Rhodes, M (2001) 'The Political Economy of Social Pacts: 'Competitive Corporatism' and European Welfare Reform', in Pierson, P (ed.) *The New Politics of the Welfare State* (Oxford: Oxford University Press) pp 165-194.

Scharpf, F (1997) 'European Integration, Democracy and the Welfare State', *Journal of European Public Policy* 4 (1): pp 18-36.

Siedentop, L (2000) *Democracy in Europe* (Harmondsworth: Allen Lane/ Penguin Press).

Leading Economies Compared

Table 1.1: Population, Labour Force and Unemployment, 2001

	Population (millions)	Civilian Labour Force (as per cent of population)	Unemployment (as per cent of civilian labour force)
France	60.9	43.4	8.8
Germany	82.3	48.3	8.0
Italy	57.9	40.7	9.6
UK	58.8	49.9	4.8
EUI5	379.4	46.1	7.5
US	285.9	49.6	4.8
Japan	127.2	53.1	5.0

Table 1.2: Gross Domestic Product per Head, Level (2001) and Rate of Growth (1970-2001)

	Level, 2001[18] (US dollars)	Average annual per cent change[19] 1970-1989	1990-2001
France	26,179	2.3	1.4
Germany	26,321	2.3	1.4
Italy	26,165	2.7	1.4
UK	26,226	2.2	2.0
EUI5	25,532	2.3	1.7
US	35,045	2.2	1.7
Japan	26,416	3.2	1.0

Output per head of population is about one third higher in the US than in the other leading economies, while in 2001, at the peak of the boom, the US unemployment rate was only two thirds the EU average. However, the US employs a higher fraction of its population in producing goods and services than continental European countries and, on average, US workers work longer hours than their French and German counterparts. Consequently, output *per hour worked* is lower in the US than in France and Germany. All countries experienced a slowdown in the *growth* of output per head during the 1990s, but this was particularly marked in Japan, which fell from the top of the growth league to the bottom.

Table 1.3: Numbers unemployed as per cent of civilian labour force, averages for various periods, 1974-2001

	1974-1983	1984-1993	1994-2001
France	5.7	10.0	11.2
Germany	4.2	7.2	8.7
Italy	7.2	11.0	11.2
UK	6.1	9.2	7.0
EU15	6.0	9.7	9.9
US	7.4	6.4	4.9
Japan	2.1	2.5	3.9

Table 1.4: Civilian employment, percentage change, 1979-2001

	1979-1990	1991-2001
France	3.2	9.1
Germany	10.3	−0.8
Italy	5.8	−0.5
UK	6.9	6.3
EU15	8.2	6.2
US	20.2	14.7
Japan	14.1	0.7

US unemployment rates used to exceed those of Western Europe and Japan. Over the past twenty years, however, the US has, in general, been more successful in generating jobs and reducing joblessness. In Japan employment remained static during the 1990s, while in Germany and Italy it actually declined. On the other hand, as stressed in the text, several small European countries have even better records than the US in creating new jobs and maintaining or re-attaining low unemployment rates.

Sources for Tables 1.1, 1.3 and 1.4: OECD (2002) *Labour Force Statistics* 1981-2001 (Paris: OECD); for Table 1.2: OECD (2003) *National Accounts of OECD Countries* (Paris: OECD).

[18] Measured at current prices and current purchasing power parities.
[19] Calculated from figures for GDP measured at constant (1995) prices and purchasing power parities.

The European Union: Membership, History and Institutions

2.1 EU Membership

Current Member States with dates of accession

Belgium, France, Germany, Italy, Luxembourg, Netherlands	1957
Denmark, Ireland, UK	1973
Greece	1981
Portugal, Spain	1986
Austria, Finland, Sweden	1995

Candidate Members

- **Due to join in 2004:**
  Czech Republic, Hungary, Poland, Slovakia, Slovenia, Estonia, Latvia, Lithuania, Cyprus, Malta

- **Engaged in accession negotiations:**
  Bulgaria, Romania

- **Due to begin accession negotiations in 2005:**
  Turkey

2.2 Transnational economic integration: a stylised gradation

Exclusive national sovereignty over money, trade and fiscal policy

+ removal of tariffs and quotas on intra-union trade
= *Free Trade Area*

+ common external tariff on imports from outside union
= *Customs Union*

+ free internal movement of capital, labour and enterprise
= *Common Market*

+ single currency, joint central bank and agreed rules for national fiscal policy
= *Economic and Monetary Union* (EMU)

+ tax harmonisation and powers for union authorities to raise taxes and issue bonds to finance union spending programmes, subject to parliamentary approval
= *Federal State*

Points to note:

1. When France, Germany, Italy and the Benelux countries formed the *European Community* (EC) under the *Treaty of Rome* in 1957, they set out to create a Common Market, as defined above. This phase in the development of what is now the EU was completed by 1969, but it was not until the *Single European Act* of 1986 that Member States took the final step towards establishing borderless markets, and not until 1999 that they made the transition to EMU.

2. The process of economic integration is neither inevitable nor irreversible and each stage has required the agreement of EU Member States. At present, there is little support – and, indeed,

no need – for the far-reaching fiscal changes that would be required to transform the EU into a federal European state.

2.3 Recent historical landmarks

1978: European Currency Unit (Ecu) and Exchange Rate
    Mechanism (ERM) created
    The Ecu, composed of a basket of EC currencies in fixed proportions, served as a Community unit of account and as an anchor for the ERM. Member States participating in the ERM undertook to keep the rates at which their currencies exchanged, both against each other and against the Ecu, within certain margins either side of agreed parities. Any government having trouble holding its position within the grid could seek its partners' consent to an exchange rate realignment.

1979: First direct elections to the European Parliament

1986: Single European Act
    Aimed at removing non-tariff barriers to the free movement of goods within the EC. Its architect, Jacques Delors, then President of the Commission, sought to use the Act as a springboard for a union-wide social policy, arguing that if the ECwas to have a single 'economic space', its citizens should also enjoy a common body of social rights and standards. Efforts to this end were, however, strongly resisted by the UK, and the resulting *Social Charter*, subsequently incorporated as the *Social Chapter* of the Maastricht Treaty, was purely declaratory, largely non-contentious and applied to *workers* rather than *citizens*.

1988-9: Delors Report on EMU
    Proposed a three-stage programme for moving to full monetary union. In Stage I, from 1990 to 1993, Member

States would complete the single market programme – including the liberalisation of capital movements – and join the ERM on uniform terms. In Stage II, they would work towards 'economic convergence', as judged by specified *financial* criteria rather than by 'real' economic indicators such as per capita income or unemployment rates.

1991-3: Treaty on European Union
Signed at Maastricht in December 1991 and eventually ratified during 1992-3, though in the case of Denmark only after two referenda. Member States agreed to establish a single currency by 1 January 1999 – the UK was allowed to opt-out – and to develop two additional 'pillars' of inter-governmental collaboration: a common foreign and security policy and co-operation on 'justice and home affairs'. The Treaty also introduced a *Co-decision Procedure* which enlarged and strengthened the legislative role of the European Parliament, hitherto largely consultative, real power residing with the Council of Ministers.

1992-3: International currency turmoil
In September 1992, speculative pressure forced the British and Italian governments to leave the ERM and 'float' their currencies, while Ireland, Portugal and Spain were forced to realign within the ERM. In July 1993, the narrow-margin ERM was abandoned and the permitted margin of fluctuation temporarily widened to 15%.

December 1995: *Euro* adopted as name for single currency

December 1996: *Stability and Growth Pact* agreed.
Member States agreed to observe certain fiscal rules, pledging – notably – not to allow public borrowing to exceed 3% of GDP in any one year.

December 1997: Treaty of Amsterdam
The Co-decision Procedure introduced at Maastricht was simplified and extended to new policy areas; the principle of *subsidiarity* was formally incorporated into the EU's treaty base; the post of *High Representative for Common Foreign and Security Policy* was established.

May 1998: First-wave entrants to euro-zone decided
11 Member States were deemed to have met the Maastricht convergence criteria and opted to join the single currency; Denmark, Sweden and the UK opted to stay out; Greece failed to qualify for entry at this time, but gained admission later.

June 1998: European Central Bank established

January 1999: Euro launched
The conversion rates of euro-zone currencies were fixed irrevocably and the euro became a currency in its own right.

March 1999: European Commission resigned *en bloc*
Commission President, Jacques Santer, and 19 Commissioners resigned after a critical report of Independent Experts investigating allegations of sleaze and mismanagement. Romano Prodi was asked to form a new Commission.

December 2000: Treaty of Nice
After much wrangling, elected Heads of State and Government agreed on institutional reforms aimed at facilitating EU enlargement: notably, the extension of *Qualified Majority Voting* to new policy areas; the reform of the Commission, each Member State having only one Commissioner after 2005 and a system of rotation coming into use once the EU has 27 members; a new method of voting in the Council, requiring a 'triple majority' – of population, of Member States and a qualified majority of votes – for legislation to be adopted; and an enlargement of the European Parliament, from 626 Members to 732.

January 2002: Euro banknotes and coins introduced.

December 2002: Accession negotiations with ten candidate countries concluded.

2.4 EU policy-making: key institutions

The European Council

- Consists of the Commission President, elected Heads of State and Government and Foreign Ministers.

- Meets routinely twice a year, with a rotating presidency.

- Has no formal law-making role: provides general political direction, resolving deadlock and prescribing guidelines.

The Council of Ministers

- The EU's ultimate authority, though on a wide range of issues it now shares legislative powers with the European Parliament.

- Comprises one minister from each Member State. Ministers represent their respective governments and are accountable to their national parliaments.

- Composition varies according to the issues under discussion – foreign affairs, economics and finance, agriculture etc.

- Voting procedure: for reserved issues, including taxes and employment law, unanimity is required, but majority voting is the norm. Unless otherwise specified, a simple majority suffices, each Council member having one vote. However, the Treaties also provide for Qualified Majority Voting where Member States' votes are weighted on the basis of their populations and corrected in favour of the smaller countries: e.g. France, Germany, Italy and the UK have 10 votes each, Luxembourg has 2. The threshold for a majority is currently 62 votes out of 87.

The European Commission

- Currently comprises 20 Commissioners (two each from the big five states), appointed for four-year renewable terms, each with a specific portfolio.

- Commissioners can be removed *en bloc*, but not individually, by the European Parliament.

- Supported by a staff of 16,000 allocated among various Directorates-General and specialist services.

- Serves as the EU bureaucracy, guardian of the EU Treaties and dynamo of the 'European project'.

- Initiates legislation; mediates conflicts in Council; implements, monitors and enforces EU laws. More generally, seeks to set agendas, influence opinion, build coalitions and broker agreements among other policy actors.

The European Parliament

- Directly elected in each Member State under national voting systems.

- MEPs form union-wide groupings out of national contingents.

- Works mainly through specialist committees.

- In some policy areas, co-legislates with the Council; in other areas, must be consulted about proposals emanating from the Council.

The Economic and Social Committee

- Consists of representatives of employers' associations, trade unions, professions, farmers, consumer groups and other organised interests.

- Contains 222 members, drawn from Member States according to quota and appointed by the Council following proposals made by national governments.

- Enjoys extensive consultative rights in relation to EU legislation and serves as a sounding board for Commission initiatives.

- Provided a model for the similarly constituted *Committee of the Regions*, created in 1992, which brings together representatives of EU regions and local authorities.

- Exemplifies a consensual, liberal-corporatist approach to policy-making which is taken for granted in other EU states, but has enjoyed a more tenuous existence in the UK and was firmly repudiated by the Thatcher governments of the 1980s.

The European Court of Justice

- Not, strictly speaking, a policy-making body: interprets and upholds the EU's legal framework by ruling on cases brought before it and cannot issue judgments unless cases are referred. Nevertheless, specific judgments have strengthened the EU's supranational character by establishing that EU law takes precedence over national law and confers rights and duties which national courts must enforce.

Some other books published by **LUATH** PRESS

POLITICS & CURRENT ISSUES

Scotlands of the Future
introduced and edited by
Eurig Scandrett
ISBN 1 84282 035 4 PB £7.99

Scotlands of the Mind
Angus Calder
ISBN 1 84282 008 7 PB £9.99

Trident on Trial: the case for people's disarmament
Angie Zelter
ISBN 1 84282 004 4 PB £9.99

Uncomfortably Numb: A Prison Requiem
Maureen Maguire
ISBN 1 84282 001 X PB £8.99

Scotland: Land & Power – the Agenda for Land Reform
Andy Wightman
ISBN 0 946487 70 7 PB £5.00

Old Scotland New Scotland
Jeff Fallow
ISBN 0 946487 40 5 PB £6.99

Some Assembly Required: behind the scenes at the re-birth of the Scottish Parliament
David Shepherd
ISBN 0 946487 84 7 PB £7.99

Notes from the North
Emma Wood
ISBN 0 946487 46 4 PB £8.99

NATURAL WORLD

The Hydro Boys: pioneers of renew-able energy
Emma Wood
ISBN 1 84282 016 8 HB £16.99

Wild Scotland
James McCarthy
photographs by Laurie Campbell
ISBN 0 946487 37 5 PB £8.99

Wild Lives: Otters – On the Swirl of the Tide
Bridget MacCaskill
ISBN 0 946487 67 7 PB £9.99

Wild Lives: Foxes – The Blood is Wild
Bridget MacCaskill
ISBN 0 946487 71 5 PB £9.99

Scotland – Land & People: An Inhabited Solitude
James McCarthy
ISBN 0 946487 57 X PB £7.99

The Highland Geology Trail
John L Roberts
ISBN 0 946487 36 7 PB £4.99

'Nothing but Heather!'
Gerry Cambridge
ISBN 0 946487 49 9 PB £15.00

Red Sky at Night
John Barrington
ISBN 0 946487 60 X PB £8.99

Listen to the Trees
Don MacCaskill
ISBN 0 946487 65 0 PB £9.99

THE QUEST FOR

The Quest for the Celtic Key
Karen Ralls-MacLeod and
Ian Robertson
ISBN 0 946487 73 1 HB £18.99

The Quest for Arthur
Stuart McHardy
ISBN 1 842820 12 5 HB £16.99

The Quest for the Nine Maidens
Stuart McHardy
ISBN 0 946487 66 9 HB £16.99

ON THE TRAIL OF

On the Trail of the Pilgrim Fathers
J. Keith Cheetham
ISBN 0 946487 83 9 PB £7.99

On the Trail of Mary Queen of Scots
J. Keith Cheetham
ISBN 0 946487 50 2 PB £7.99

On the Trail of John Wesley
J. Keith Cheetham
ISBN 1 84282 023 0 PB £7.99

On the Trail of William Wallace
David R. Ross
ISBN 0 946487 47 2 PB £7.99

On the Trail of Robert the Bruce
David R. Ross
ISBN 0 946487 52 9 PB £7.99

On the Trail of Robert Service
GW Lockhart
ISBN 0 946487 24 3 PB £7.99

On the Trail of John Muir
Cherry Good
ISBN 0 946487 62 6 PB £7.99

On the Trail of Robert Burns
John Cairney
ISBN 0 946487 51 0 PB £7.99

On the Trail of Bonnie Prince Charlie
David R Ross
ISBN 0 946487 68 5 PB £7.99

On the Trail of Robert Burns
John Cairney
ISBN 0 946487 51 0 PB £7.99

On the Trail of Queen Victoria in the Highlands
Ian R Mitchell
ISBN 0 946487 79 0 PB £7.99

ISLANDS

The Islands that Roofed the World: Easdale, Belnahua, Luing & Seil:
Mary Withall
ISBN 0 946487 76 6 PB £4.99

Rum: Nature's Island
Magnus Magnusson
ISBN 0 946487 32 4 PB £7.95

LUATH GUIDES TO SCOTLAND

The North West Highlands: Roads to the Isles
Tom Atkinson
ISBN 0 946487 54 5 PB £4.95

Mull and Iona: Highways and Byways
Peter Macnab
ISBN 0 946487 58 8 PB £4.95

The Northern Highlands: The Empty Lands
Tom Atkinson
ISBN 0 946487 55 3 PB £4.95

The West Highlands: The Lonely Lands
Tom Atkinson
ISBN 0 946487 56 1 PB £4.95

South West Scotland
Tom Atkinson
ISBN 0 946487 04 9 PB £4.95

TRAVEL & LEISURE

Die Kleine Schottlandfibel [Scotland Guide in German]
Hans-Walter Arends
ISBN 0 946487 89 8 PB £8.99

Let's Explore Edinburgh Old Town
Anne Bruce English
ISBN 0 946487 98 7 PB £4.99

Edinburgh's Historic Mile
Duncan Priddle
ISBN 0 946487 97 9 PB £2.99

Pilgrims in the Rough: St Andrews beyond the 19th hole
Michael Tobert
ISBN 0 946487 74 X PB £7.99

FOOD & DRINK

The Whisky Muse: Scotch whisky in poem & song
various, ed. Robin Laing
ISBN 0 946487 95 2 PB £12.99

First Foods Fast: how to prepare good simple meals for your baby
Lara Boyd
ISBN 1 84282 002 8 PB £4.99

Edinburgh and Leith Pub Guide
Stuart McHardy
ISBN 0 946487 80 4 PB £4.95

WALK WITH LUATH

Skye 360: walking the coastline of Skye
Andrew Dempster
ISBN 0 946487 85 5 PB £8.99

Walks in the Cairngorms
Ernest Cross
ISBN 0 946487 09 X PB £4.95

Short Walks in the Cairngorms
Ernest Cross
ISBN 0 946487 23 5 PB £4.95

The Joy of Hillwalking
Ralph Storer
ISBN 0 946487 28 6 PB £7.50

Scotland's Mountains before the Mountaineers
Ian R Mitchell
ISBN 0 946487 39 1 PB £9.99

Mountain Days & Bothy Nights
Dave Brown & Ian R Mitchell
ISBN 0 946487 15 4 PB £7.50

SPORT

Ski & Snowboard Scotland
Hilary Parke
ISBN 0 946487 35 9 PB £6.99

Over the Top with the Tartan Army
Andy McArthur
ISBN 0 946487 45 6 PB £7.99

BIOGRAPHY

The Last Lighthouse
Sharma Krauskopf
ISBN 0 946487 96 0 PB £7.99

Tobermory Teuchter
Peter Macnab
ISBN 0 946487 41 3 PB £7.99

Bare Feet & Tackety Boots
Archie Cameron
ISBN 0 946487 17 0 PB £7.95

Come Dungeons Dark
John Taylor Caldwell
ISBN 0 946487 19 7 PB £6.95

HISTORY

Civil Warrior
Robin Bell
ISBN 1 84282 013 3 HB £10.99

A Passion for Scotland
David R Ross
ISBN 1 84282 019 2 PB £5.99

Reportage Scotland: History in the Making
Louise Yeoman
ISBN 0 946487 61 8 PB £9.99

Blind Harry's Wallace
Hamilton of Gilbertfield
introduced by Elspeth King
illustrations by Owain Kirby
ISBN 0 946487 33 2 PB £8.99

SOCIAL HISTORY

Pumpherston: the story of a shale oil village
Sybil Cavanagh
ISBN 1 84282 011 7 HB £17.99
ISBN 1 84282 015 X PB £7.99

Shale Voices
Alistair Findlay
ISBN 0 946487 78 2 HB £17.99
ISBN 0 946487 63 4 PB £10.99

A Word for Scotland
Jack Campbell
ISBN 0 946487 48 0 PB £12.99

FOLKLORE

Scotland: Myth, Legend & Folklore
Stuart McHardy
ISBN 0 946487 69 3 PB £7.99

Luath Storyteller: Highland Myths & Legends
George W Macpherson
ISBN 1 84282 003 6 PB £5.00

Tales of the North Coast
Alan Temperley
ISBN 0 946487 18 9 PB £8.99

Tall Tales from an Island
Peter Macnab
ISBN 0 946487 07 3 PB £8.99

The Supernatural Highlands
Francis Thompson
ISBN 0 946487 31 6 PB £8.99

GENEALOGY

Scottish Roots: step-by-step guide for ancestor hunters
Alwyn James
ISBN 1 84282 007 9 PB £9.99

WEDDINGS, MUSIC AND DANCE

The Scottish Wedding Book
G Wallace Lockhart
ISBN 1 94282 010 9 PB £12.99

Fiddles & Folk
G Wallace Lockhart
ISBN 0 946487 38 3 PB £7.95

Highland Balls & Village Halls
G Wallace Lockhart
ISBN 0 946487 12 X PB £6.95

POETRY

Bad Ass Raindrop
Kokumo Rocks
ISBN 1 84282 018 4 PB £6.99

Caledonian Cramboclink: verse, broadsheets and in conversation
William Neill
ISBN 0 946487 53 7 PB £8.99

Men and Beasts: wild men & tame animals
Val Gillies & Rebecca Marr
ISBN 0 946487 92 8 PB £15.00

The Luath Burns Companion
John Cairney
ISBN 1 84282 000 1 PB £10.00

Scots Poems to be read aloud
introduced Stuart McHardy
ISBN 0 946487 81 2 PB £5.00

Poems to be read aloud
introduced by Tom Atkinson
ISBN 0 946487 00 6 PB £5.00

Picking Brambles and Other Poems
Des Dillon
ISBN 1 84282 021 4 PB £6.99

Kate o Shanter's Tale and Other Poems
Matthew Fitt
ISBN 1 84282 028 1 PB £6.99

CARTOONS

Broomie Law
Cinders McLeod
ISBN 0 946487 99 5 PB £4.00

FICTION

The Road Dance
John MacKay
ISBN 1 84282 024 9 PB £9.99

Milk Treading
Nick Smith
ISBN 0 946487 75 8 PB £9.99

The Strange Case of RL Stevenson
Richard Woodhead
ISBN 0 946487 86 3 HB £16.99

But n Ben A-Go-Go
Matthew Fitt
ISBN 1 84282 014 1 PB £6.99
ISBN 0 946487 82 0 HB £10.99

Grave Robbers
Robin Mitchell
ISBN 0 946487 72 3 PB £7.99

The Bannockburn Years
William Scott
ISBN 0 946487 34 0 PB £7.95

The Great Melnikov
Hugh MacLachlan
ISBN 0 946487 42 1 PB £7.95

The Fundamentals of New Caledonia
David Nicol
ISBN 0 946487 93 6 HB £16.99

LANGUAGE

Luath Scots Language Learner [Book]
L Colin Wilson
ISBN 0 946487 91 X PB £9.99

Luath Scots Language Learner [Double Audio CD Set]
L Colin Wilson
ISBN 1 84282 026 5 CD £16.99

Luath Press Limited

committed to publishing well written books worth reading

LUATH PRESS takes its name from Robert Burns, whose little collie Luath (*Gael.*, swift or nimble) tripped up Jean Armour at a wedding and gave him the chance to speak to the woman who was to be his wife and the abiding love of his life. Burns called one of *The Twa Dogs* Luath after Cuchullin's hunting dog in *Ossian's Fingal*. Luath Press was established in 1981 in the heart of Burns country, and is now based a few steps up the road from Burns' first lodgings on Edinburgh's Royal Mile.

Luath offers you distinctive writing with a hint of unexpected pleasures.

Most bookshops either carry our books in stock or can order them for you. To order direct from us, please send a £sterling cheque, postal order, international money order or your credit card details (number, address of cardholder and expiry date) to us at the address below. Please add post and packing as follows: UK – £1.00 per delivery address; overseas surface mail – £2.50 per delivery address; overseas airmail – £3.50 for the first book to each delivery address, plus £1.00 for each additional book by airmail to the same address. If your order is a gift, we will happily enclose your card or message at no extra charge.

Luath Press Limited
543/2 Castlehill
The Royal Mile
Edinburgh EH1 2ND
Scotland
Telephone: 0131 225 4326 (24 hours)
Fax: 0131 225 4324
email: gavin.macdougall@luath.co.uk
Website: www.luath.co.uk